Preparing Inventions for Marketing Success

The Secrets of Successful Inventors

by: James M. Lowrance © 2010

SECTION ONE: "Marketing Inventions Successfully" (Pages 7 through 56)

SECTION TWO: "The Best Darn Invention Marketing Book!" (Pages 57 through 109)

INTRODUCTION:

This book being a combination of two previously published titles ("Marketing Inventions Successfully" and "The Best Darn Invention Marketing eBook!"), provides inventors with essential facts, considerations and steps that must be implemented before launching new product-inventions onto the marketplace, to better increase the odds for success. Authored by inventor - Jim Lowrance, who has successfully marketed and licensed six products in the outdoors sports industry, placing them with some of the world's largest retail outlets, including Wal-Mart stores, Bass Pro Shops and Cabela's.

He also gained national telemarketing exposure for his products and landed a national promotion for his patented fishing rod accessory called "The Rod Floater", with a major oil company - Kerr-McGee, manufacturer of Mystik outboard motor oil (1992). He currently still receives royalty payments for this invention (since 1995) and previously licensed five others, eventually selling them for outright sums to manufacturers who still market them.

3

Written in easy-to-follow language, this resource offers opportunity for a well-rounded, general education that can help to instill a better level of confidence and knowledge to inventors of new products with potential for success in the marketplace. No one can promise positive outcomes to inventors but being well-armed with the right information can significantly increase the chances of success.

TABLE OF CONTENTS – SECTION ONE (6 Chapters):

"Marketing Inventions Successfully"

Chapter One: My Personal Invention Success Story

Chapter Two: Marketing Your Own Invention

Chapter Three: Patenting - Protecting Your Invention

Chapter Four: Promoting Your Invention in the Market Place

Chapter Five: The Advantages in "licensing" (Royalty Agreement) your Invention

Chapter Six: Beware of Dishonest Invention Companies

TABLE OF CONTENTS – SECTION TWO (9 Chapters):

"The Best Darn Invention Marketing Book!"

Chapter One: Researching the Market Value of Inventions

Chapter Two: Preparing for Invention Submission

Chapter Three: Conducting a Preliminary Patent Search

Chapter Four: The Valuable USPTO Provisional Patent Program

Chapter Five: Test Marketing Inventions Effectively

Chapter Six: The Invention License Agreement Option

Chapter Seven: Pursuing License Agreements for Inventions

Chapter Eight: Methods for Licensing Inventions

Chapter Nine: My Invention Marketing Success Story Revisited

Preparing Inventions for Marketing Success

It is my sincere wish that this book contributes to the success of many other inventors who help to give our world a brighter future through new and innovative inventions!

-*Jim Lowrance*

SECTION ONE:

Marketing Inventions Successfully

Increasing Odds for Inventor Success

CHAPTER ONE

My Personal Invention Success Story

In the mid 1980s, myself and my brother-in-law, both of us living in North Central Texas at the time and both being fishermen, invented a device to prevent fishing rod combos from sinking if accidentally dropped into the water. We came up with this idea after our own experiences of dropping rod combos overboard, plus the experiences of other fishermen we knew that experienced the same. This included my father-in-law who had a rod flip out of his boat while trolling, after his fishing line snagged on some brush in the lake.

Preparing Inventions for Marketing Success

We knew a fishing rod flotation device would fulfill a need and offer assurance to fishermen against losing their expensive rigs or those of sentimental value.

We were excited about the idea but first wanted to make sure it would actually work and would not be inconvenient or cumbersome if placed on a fishing rod combo. We decided that a poly foam piece would fit just above the rod handle of a fishing combo with plenty of room between it and the first eyelet on the rod. We began searching for cylinder-shaped material that could slip onto a rod and not be too large in diameter, as to interfere with the fishing line. We ended up finding some pads that fit over the crossbars of bicycles and these worked quit well but they were either black or white and we wanted bright, highly visible colors for use as prototypes for showing and demonstrating the product. We found such foam pieces that were perfect in size (strangely enough), in a toy called "Nerf Swords". These were bright yellow and orange and all that was needed, was for us to cut them to length, drill a hole down the center of them and to cut a slit-opening, to place them onto fishing rods.

These looked very nice installed on fishing rod combos and so we made a demonstration VHS video of these in use and floating in the water.

We first contracted with an invention firm in 1985 that we later discovered was not performing the duties they claimed to be and we lost nearly $5,000.00 using their bogus contract services. I was living in my current state of Oklahoma at the time and I obtained a release from the invention company. I also asked for the approval of my brother-in-law, still living in Texas, for me to pursue the marketing of our invention on my own, which we decided to call the "Rod Floater". He gave me the okay to market it from my location and so I decided to get some investors involved, who could help finance the product's patenting and development.

I was able to secure three investors, including my own father, who agreed to invest operating capitol, into the project, that would get the product patented, set up for manufacturing locally, insured and packaged. In other words, these men agreed to invest the money needed to get the product ready for placing on the shelves of stores.

We formed a corporation of partners in this endeavor, that we titled "Low-Mac, Inc." and with the funds invested, we first applied for a design patent, which was granted within two years of submission to the USPTO (U.S. Patent & Trademark Office). We were able to start our marketing campaign much earlier however because once a "patent pending" is achieved, an invention is already protected. The current manufacturer, that now markets it, also has the product Trademark Registered.

I knew I was setting my goals high but decided my first attempt to get the product into an outlet, would be a presentation to Wal-Mart Stores. I previously mentioned a home video demo, my brother-in-law and myself made of the Rod Floaters and we used this video in our presentation to Wal-Mart buyers.

As a result, they approved us for selling the product, in a region of their stores! Not only did they contract us to sell the product to the approved stores, but most of the stores started out with an end-cap display of Rod Floaters and used our demo video, on continuous play, in their sporting goods departments!

From that moment forward, we began to add more major outlets carrying Rod Floaters, including Bass Pro Shops, Cabela's and Academy Stores, plus many other smaller chains, catalogs and independents. We also had several T.V. shows, some that were national, telemarketing the Rod Floaters. We also entered into a deal with Kerr-McGee Oil Company (Cato Division), for them to use the Rod Floater, as a promo-premium (give away item), inside all cases of "Mystik Outboard Motor Oil", in 1992, to help boost their sales. This was a very large order, with a profit built into it and very exciting times for us, seeing the product doing so well on the market.

In 1996, we decided to turn the product over to another company for marketing. My partners and I were doing this as a sideline and it became too much for us to handle!

The major fishing tackle company that we licensed the product to and the one still marketing it today, is Blakemore Corporation, in Branson MO. (the TTI-Companies Group). They have been paying us a monthly royalty check on sales, since that time, to date.

I attempted afterward, to license other products over to other companies and I developed some additional fishing and hunting products. One of the products, was a lure/hook cover for attaching to your fishing rod line that prevented hooks from snagging on things (i.e. people, car seats and carpets), while transporting and storing them. I called the product "Tube-A-Lure" and I did interest a company to take it on under a license agreement however, the product was squeezed off the market, by a number of similar products that came out, made cheaper and having reputable names on them, by major tackle manufacturers. As a result, the company discontinued its marketing attempt.

I also invented some chumming pouches that you fill with fish attractant/chum and cast them out with your fishing rod, into the area of water to be fished in, to attract fish and afterward retrieve the chum pouch for reuse. I also had similar pouches for hanging from trees, in areas for attracting deer. I made these in pre-filled versions and also pouches that were ready-to-fill, made from porous material that would leach-out these attractants and attract deer and fish.

I successfully placed these pouches in several districts of Wal-Mart stores and into some catalogs. Shortly thereafter I became ill with the onset of Autoimmune Thyroid Disease and decided to sell the products outright, to a company in Pana, IL. called "Pana Bait Company", who also publishes the "Catfish Connection" catalog. This company, like Blakemore, is still marketing the pouches but being an outright sale to them and not a license agreement, they do not owe us an ongoing royalty on sales.

In the year 2001, Inventor's Digest did a feature article about my invention experiences that they published in their May/June issue.

Bass Pro Shops online link to the "Rod Floater">> http://reviews.basspro.com/2010/16517/reviews.htm

CHAPTER TWO

Marketing Your Own Invention

The steps I will discuss following, will give an inventor a general idea of the process for marketing a product-invention. These steps should follow those that have already been completed for protecting and patenting an invention (see Chapter Three), so that it is ready for public disclosure.

Incorporate

With the possible risks of "product liability" and patent lawsuits, an inventor should "incorporate", meaning form a corporation or form a "Limited Liability Company" (LLC) so that you become a corporate entity or company and not remain a liable individual. This may seem like a strange step but it is a necessary one, in order to reduce the risk of someone pursuing you as an individual for patent infringement, or to contest your patent, or for product liability, meaning an injury lawsuit from use of your product.

While these possibilities of being sued are statistically small, they do happen and if you form a corporation of partners, the corporation becomes a separate entity from you. If a lawsuit were to be filed, whether real or imagined (frivolous), the party suing would have to go after the assets of the corporation, rather than your personal assets. This offers you some protection by forming a corporation or LLC which in addition to being separate legal entities, they are also offered certain protections under the law and important benefits as well.

If you need partners to invest in the marketing of your invention, for a percentage of ownership, these investors can become your corporate partners or "officers of the corporation". If you do not need investors, you can simply form a corporation with family members and/or friends. You will need to check with an attorney in your city or find an agent online who sets up corporations in your state. This person will help you file your articles of incorporation (includes naming officers) and help you get approval for your business name, through your state's corporations office.

The fee to incorporate can range from $100.00 to $800.00, depending on the state where you incorporate.

Research

Find out details of what it will take to manufacture your product-invention, such as tooling, molding, warehousing and labor. That way, you can determine whether you can feasibly manufacture it or instead will need to contract a company to manufacture it for you. This is one of the more difficult steps because of the research it requires.

You need to determine what materials and manufacturing machinery you will need to make your invention. For each piece of material or machinery needed, you should contact several sources to get the best prices possible. If you can get by with a barn or a garage at first to use as your manufacturing facility and warehouse, this too is a consideration; having to build a facility can be a very large expense. Another consideration when establishing a manufacturing/warehousing facility is to look into the possibility of renting a building.

Once you have looked at all of the combined expenses for manufacturing your product, you can from there decide if it is more in your interest to do so yourself, or to contract a manufacturer to do so for you. Some manufacturers who already have the machinery will only charge you a per-unit price for completed units of your product. This can sometimes be the most cost effective way to go with manufacturing an invention.

Design Appealing Packaging

Packaging has a great deal to do with how well your product will sell. An inventor and his partners should come up with a basic design for packaging their product and possibly look at several variations of how to use the design. The design itself would be your picture(s) and wording on your package and how it is laid out. The variation of it would be the type container you use.

Some products can be placed into a plastic bag, with a header card at the top that is stapled on, while others need to be in a box with the design on the outside of it.

There are also "clam shell" packages or what are also called "blister-packs", but these are somewhat more expensive because they are plastic pieces, molded by a manufacturer and they usually require you to order large minimums of these. An inventor must decide which of these types of packaging are most cost effective for their invention because the added expense of packaging will affect the final retail of the product.

When designing the packaging, an inventor should have the goal of making the design eye-catching and appealing but not go overboard and make the design look like an overkill (gaudy). There is a psychology to package design and the goal is to increase sales by attracting consumers to your product.

Secure Product Liability Insurance

This step insures that if you have a lawsuit filed against you, by a user of your product, you are covered by your product liability insurance. How dangerous or threatening your product is, or how non-threatening and safe it is, determines the cost of your insurance premiums (cost for coverage).

For example, if an inventor's product is something that improves the performance of a firearm, this could increase insurance premiums considerably.

However, if an inventor's product is a new type of pillow to make an easy chair more comfortable, the premiums on the product liability policy will likely be very low.

Product liability insurance is usually coverage of at least $1,000,000.00. However, depending upon the product being covered your monthly insurance premiums might not exceed $50.00 to $100.00 per month.

There are retail stores and outlets that require their vendors to carry product liability insurance or they will not consider carrying their products.

This is true of the major chains as well, including Wal-Marts and Target Stores, Bass Pro Shops etc… Based on all expenses to market your product set your distributor and wholesale price, so that you make the amount of profit you need.

Set your Price

After you have researched everything and have a very firm price on everything required to manufacture your product, from there you will be able to set your price for making a profit.

With all expenses figured into manufacturing finished units, you need to add your profit-percentage on top of that, so that you are making the profit needed when selling to distributors and retailers.

Distributors are companies who buy from manufacturers and resell the product to retailers. You will also likely sell to retailers yourself. Distributors usually need approximately 30% markup, when selling to retailers.

Retailers usually need to make approximately 40% when they sell your product to consumers. You need to set your price to either, so that you are making the percentage of profit you need but that will also keep the retail at an affordable amount for the end-use consumer.

Establish Sales Appeal and a Sales Track Record

These items will increase the interest of retail outlets for buying your product. This step involves finding ways to show how sale-able your product is. You can do this by offering your product for sale through magazine ads, online, at booth shows, via a television commercial or by selling it in a number of stores as a test-market. When using any of these methods, you want to promote your product the best you possibly can, in order to have the best possible recorded sales to present to retail outlets you approach to carry your product.

If this results in stores carrying your product, you continue to record the sales you get through new outlets and this gives you an ongoing record of your product's sales appeal. Over time, a successful sales track record will continue to help you expand into larger outlets and chain stores.

While the above steps are somewhat simplified, they give a general idea of what is involved in getting an invention marketed.

Some inventors do not desire to go through this complicated process and so will instead pursue a "Licensing Agreement" for their invention. This is a contract that grants rights to a manufacturer to manufacture and sell an invention and pay the inventor a royalty percentage. Manufacturing an invention on your own will bring a larger profit percentage because royalties are relatively small in comparison. But all duties are the inventor's to perform. With a licensing, the manufacturing/marketing company performs all the duties for you.

CHAPTER THREE

Patenting - Protecting Your Invention

When you conceive an invention that you feel might be marketable, there are steps you can take that will help you to determine whether it is. If you proceed with an invention, before taking these steps, you may be setting yourself up for disappointment by going forward with an idea that is already out there and that you cannot obtain a patent for.

My experience in this area comes from marketing and licensing six of my own inventions, beginning in 1989. I was able to establish five of these on the market by getting them into Wal-Mart stores. Then I turned them over to companies who could take over manufacturing and marketing and pay me a royalty on sales.

My most successful invention, the "Rod Floater," a fishing rod flotation device, was picked up by Wal-Mart, Bass Pro Shops, Cabela's and Academy Stores.

It was also used as a promotional product by Kerr-McGee Oil Company and telemarketed on a number of national TV shows. I still receive a monthly royalty to this day, after licensing the Rod Floater to a large, reputable fishing tackle company in 1996 (TTI-Blakemore Corporation).

I did lose one product invention to theft by the buyer of a large retail chain. I submitted it to the buyer without patent protection, which was a mistake. I also lost an invention to competition of other companies (who had similar products) that squeezed mine off the market. It is because of these two negative experiences that I believe taking the steps below is so important.

Look in stores and catalogs to see if the invention is already on the market.

This is a very basic, but necessary, step. It can keep you from taking further unnecessary steps or help you confirm that your invention is marketable. Look for your product on the shelves of stores, especially major retail outlet stores, and in major catalogs that carry products that are in your invention's category.

If you find the invention already on the market, you need to stop your efforts on that invention and begin working on another idea you can pursue in its place. Don't let this stop you from trying to market a new idea.

If you don't find your new invention on store shelves and in catalogs, you need to ensure that a patent hasn't already been applied for, for a similar product, via the next step listed below.

Do an online "patent search" to check for patents on same or similar inventions.

Although you might not find your invention already being marketed on store shelves or in catalogs, it's still possible that someone has applied for a patent on a similar invention but has not launched it onto the market yet.

You can do a patent search on search engines first, as a basic second step. Simply name your invention's purpose in several different combinations of search words.

For example, if your invention is a new type of dog collar that serves some type of unique purpose, describe this purpose in your search terms. There are many patent-viewing type websites now available that have helped get U.S. patents indexed highly on all of the search engines. If that doesn't yield any results, you should go to the "U.S. Patent & Trademark Office" (USPTO) website and do a more thorough search. At the USPTO site, you can rule out the possibility of infringing (copycat product) on another existing patent or patent pending (applied for and awaiting approval).

Mail an outline of your invention to yourself or have your invention witnessed by someone in writing.

This method is simply to give your invention a "date of originality." By mailing a detailed description of your invention to yourself in a plainly postmarked and sealed, self-addressed stamped envelope, or by having a friend or relative you trust sign a document stating that he or she witnessed your invention on a specific date.

You'll get an official "date of conception" by doing this.

This does not protect an invention, but gives a date that can be referred to in case another invention applies for a patent pending close to or on the same date. While this is rare, it does occasionally happen and patent attorneys refer to this scenario as "inventions being in interference," meaning the patent applications were applied for at dates very close together.

In these types of rare cases, a "date of conception" document can be referred to and will help establish the earliest date of conception. The inventor who has this would likely be the one allowed to receive the patent pending status on their invention.

Obtain a "patent pending" so that you can proceed with marketing under a protected status.

It is valuable to apply for a patent on your invention because this immediately puts it under "patent pending" status.

With a patent pending, you are allowed by U.S. Patent Law to place this term on your packaging and sales materials. A patent pending is not an approved patent, but protects your invention because your date of application prevents someone else from coming in behind you and applying for a patent on the same or a similar invention.

The USPTO has a program called the "Provisional Patent Program" and many inventors are not aware of the revised version of this program. Under this recently revised program, an inventor (small entity) can apply for a provisional patent, for a cost of $110.00 (cost as of year 2009). Once applied for, an inventor has one full year to test the market with his invention and follow up by completing the patenting process for that invention. This is a valuable program since completing a patent can cost several thousand dollars. This program allows time to see if a patent is worthwhile on a particular invention.

These are steps to help you establish the value of your invention and to get the necessary protection for it.

Once you have done this, you can then pursue marketing the product/invention yourself or you can pursue getting a "License Agreement" for it. A license agreement is a contract you enter into with a manufacturing/marketing company that can perform these duties and simply pay you a percentage of the sales.

Conducting a Patent Search

A patent search can be important for a new product-invention because it can confirm the originality of the idea or reveal that it has already been marketed or protected under a previous patent application.

Following is a brief recap of the preceding information (the 3 most important steps) regarding the obtaining of protection for your intellectual property.

Remember to first search the shelves of major department stores.
As previously stated, this step isn't actually part of a patent search, it is a step that may help confirm the value in conducting one.

Checking stores may also confirm that a patent search would not be necessary, if you discover the invention has already been successfully marketed by someone else. As a first step in establishing the originality of your product invention, it's a good idea to make sure a product is not already widely available in major chain stores or even in major catalog outlets.

You're then ready to conduct a search on major search engines.

This is that second preparatory step that helps you to get ready for conducting an actual patent search at the United States Patent & Trademark Office (USPTO) website. There are websites that are not actually connected to the USPTO, yet still index patented inventions and even non-patented inventions on the search engines, as part of their services to inventors. By doing a search on the search engines, you can better establish the need to do a more detailed and thorough search on the USPTO website. I previously used the example of a new dog collar design but if for another example, you have a new type of windshield wiper for automobiles, use several variations of search terms that describe your product invention.

31

You might also include the word "patent" in that search. This step not only helps to locate any pages of patented inventions that might be similar to your invention, but also displays results on any non-patented products in general that might already be on the market. A widely marketed product might pose too much competition for your invention and might be a deciding factor against further search using the USPTO website.

Now you're ready to conduct a search on the USPTO website.

As pointed out in a previous subheading, the value in a patent search is in working toward getting patent protection for your own invention by following up with a patent application. But it also helps prevent you from infringing upon another patent which could make you legally liable.

Go online and visit the USPTO's Index to the United States Patent Classification System. This lists all inventions of every kind, in alphabetical categories.

Conducting a thorough search takes time but can be well worth the effort to establish the originality and patent-ability of your invention.

While an inventor can conduct a patent search on his own, there are also patent agents and attorneys who can assist in this for a fee. Searching online will help you locate patent search assistance. This concludes the recap of the 3 most important steps toward protection of your intellectual property, by getting an invention ready for a patent pending submission; let us now move on to other aspects to consider.

What is the provisional Patent Program?

The USPTO "Provisional Patent Program" is a valuable program that allows inventors patent protection for one year while they develop their invention and establish its value, before investing in a more permanent type patent. This is an important way to help inventors have more money available for invention development, rather than having to have more up-front money to invest in their patents, before having the opportunity to test-market their inventions.

The provisional patent program is an affordable program offered to inventors by the USPTO.

The updated provisional patent program has in a sense replaced a former program discontinued by the USPTO that was called the "Disclosure Document Program". A provisional patent offers a trial period of market-testing and selling your invention, before you follow through with one of three more permanent types of patents, which include a design patent (design for an article of manufacture); an industrial patent (a new and useful process of manufacture or composition of matter); or a plant patent (new asexually produced variety of plant).

A provisional patent protects your invention with full patent protection and allows you to place the "patent pending" notation on your packaging.

Formerly, when inventors sent their invention description in to the USPTO under the disclosure document program, they would do so to establish a "date of conception", meaning proof of the date in which they established having invented it.

This program, however, was not a protection for the invention as the provisional patent is and did not allow the inventor to place the patent pending notation on their invention and its packaging. This is the advantage the affordable provisional patent has over this other former low cost program. **The cost to "small entities" to secure a one year provisional patent is $110.00 as of the year 2009.**

The USPTO offers this provisional patent to small entities, meaning an individual or company that has less than 500 employees, for a nominal fee of only $110.00 (please check the USPTO website for price updates). This is a very cost-effective price because you are allowed to test market and sell your invention for one year after notification that they have received and accepted your application.

If during the one year, an inventor discovers that the invention does not merit following through with a more permanent patent, at a greater cost, he can allow the term to expire and forfeit the option to follow through with a further patenting process.

The provisional patent program is valuable in that an inventor can limit the amount invested in a patent should he choose to, or he can follow through in obtaining a longer term patent.

If, during the year grace period, an inventor decides his invention is not worth obtaining a longer term patent for it (most are 14 years in duration), he can simply allow the provisional patent to lapse and he will have no further patenting costs. If, however, the value of the invention is proven during that year period, the inventor may choose to invest further into the patenting process and obtain a more permanent patent. The value of the 1-year grace period is that the worth/value of the invention can be established, without risk of theft of the inventor's product-invention. It is also valuable in that an inventor may pursue a licensing (royalty agreement) during that one year grace period and if any further patenting is done, it would be the responsibility of the licensee (one paying you royalties on sales), should the inventor secure a license agreement before the one year period has expired.

CHAPTER FOUR

Promoting Your Invention in the Market Place

Trade Shows - When you launch a new product on the market, one way to get immediate exposure to consumers is to display your product in booths at trade shows. Do a little research to find out when and where trade shows will be held that feature the type product you have; display your product at as many of these shows as possible. Booth space at these types of shows is usually very cost-effective, because it gives great exposure to your new product by allowing you to sell it directly to consumers, who will advertise for you through word-of-mouth.

Some trade shows in smaller cities offer free booth space. For those shows that are too far away or would not be within your budget to attend, you may be able to convince someone else who attends them to display your product in their booth. Ask someone who sells similar products -- they may be willing to display your product with theirs for a percentage of the sales. Or, they may split the cost of the booth space with you.

If your product creates sales and interest, they may also want to become a distributor of your product, which would be an added benefit!

Promotional Video - Simple, short-length product demonstration videos are real eye-catchers. They are great tools for using in presentations to prospective buyers, and are also effective at trade shows. People who attend these shows will gravitate toward a television screen that is playing a video.

When done properly, an amateur video can be nearly as effective as one produced professionally. If your budget does not allow for professionally produced videos, do not hesitate to produce one yourself. If you promote your product on the internet, videos can also be converted into files that are viewable online.

Promotional Fliers - It is not difficult to create quality promotional fliers that direct consumers to your product, using a computer to generate them. In today's computer age, you can create informative advertisements and print them off for disbursing in areas that will bring attention and sales to your product.

Inquire with businesses that can display them in their windows, or display a stack of them on a counter for consumers to take with them and read. Businesses you approach should be those who do not see a conflict of interest in helping you promote your product, and who might also see a benefit in doing so.

Internet Advertising - There are many websites that offer free classified ads or cost-effective paid ads. There are also blogging websites that offer free blogs (online pages under their domain) and you simply register with them, to create one. You would want to read their policies, however, to make sure they allow blogs that promote products. The great thing about a blog is that you can be as creative as you like in promoting your product. There is also website hosting available through many companies on the internet, at low cost, so that you can actually have your own domain (registered address) for a website. Website hosting can be in the $20-a-month range and up. You get access to website-building software that is high-quality and effective in promoting your new product.

Building Sales Relationships with Buyers

Always represent your product-invention with firm belief and commitment behind it. When you truly believe in the product or service you represent, this comes across in your presentations of that product to prospective buyers. Your firm belief in the product – and in its ability to fulfill a need they have for it – will be evident to the person to whom you present the product. In fact, many salespeople who are successful actually express their own strong personal belief in the product, while giving their presentation. It can also be impressive for salespeople to cite their own positive experiences with the product and/or examples of positive experiences others have had with it.

Confident and sincere representation usually works far better than high pressure selling. Some salespeople push their prospective buyer for a decision and many times this will force a "no" answer out of them. It is better instead to represent your product with sincerity and confidence, allowing the buyers to be drawn into the presentation.

They will then begin to see that the decision to buy from you is in their best interest, rather than being in your best interest. When buyers believe a salesperson is simply trying to "score a commission", this can sometimes be a turn off to them. There is a difference between being overly pushy and highly confident, and most buyers are very experienced in spotting the difference.

Create an ongoing relationship with buyers whom you successfully sell a product to. It can really impress buyers if you will follow up with them, to see how things are going with the product or service they bought from you. This can be as simple as giving them a brief phone call or e-mail to simply ask them how things are going with the product.

Over time follow-ups will help you establish an ongoing relationship with buyers so that it is easier to make future appointments to sell additional products to them. An established relationship gives you an open door of welcome to visit the buyer, rather than taking a lot more effort just to get a short meeting with them.

Observe a buyer's surroundings, to see if you find something that helps you connect better with them. When you visit buyers at their office or home, observe what types of things they have displayed in their surroundings that reveal their interests. Most people have sports or hobby type items displayed in their homes and offices, or even things such as pictures of their families that you can comment on.

By making a remark about those items, you can get a feel for whether they are eager to brag about them or to express the significance of them to you. This type of brief side-conversation can put buyers at ease because they feel a connection of like interests with you.

Salespeople have actually been known to spark such interest and friendliness through this strategy, that they will actually be invited to join the buyer in attending a sports event, for example, or in playing golf, going on a fishing trip, etc… These types of connections established with buyers, over time, can end up being lucrative relationships for a salesperson. Additionally, you can make valuable friends in the process.

When buyers have been faithful customers, send them a card or gift, to demonstrate your appreciation. Buyers are human like everyone else, despite the fact that some can be shrewd businessmen and sometimes a little tough to deal with. As human beings, they appreciate a show of your appreciation to them. You can do this by sending them a thank you card or a small gift that will express the appreciation you have for the business relationship you have with them.

This can go a long way in maintaining that relationship for the long term. Gifts that your steady buyers may appreciate are things like quality pen sets, gift certificates to nice restaurants, tie clips or cufflinks and for lady buyers, a bouquet of flowers or a gift box or perfume, with a card from your company attached.

These are steps that can help with success in selling and maintaining sales relationships, but like anything else, a salesperson also needs to have some discernment for knowing when these things will work for particular buyers and how far to go with any of these suggestions in regard to each individual.

A buyer's attitude and body language will usually indicate when you are on the right track or if you need to change your methods. Over time, a seasoned salesperson-invention representative will begin to get a feel for establishing and building relationships with buyers.

CHAPTER FIVE

The Advantages in "licensing" (Royalty Agreement) your Invention

An Inventor with a new product idea, basically has two options to choose from, in proceeding with getting an invention marketed. One option would be to actually pursue self-marketing the invention.

With this option, an Inventor will have to be responsible for every aspect of the marketing process, from top to bottom. This would include getting the invention patented or protected by other available means, such as trademark registration. It would also include getting packaging developed and produced for the product, for merchandizing it in outlets that can sell the product.

As previously discussed, an inventor would also need to either get set up to manufacture the product or secure the services of a manufacture who can produce a finished, packaged product, ready to ship to merchandisers, such as retail outlets and distributors.

There are also other odds and ends that must be completed, in order for an inventor to have a finished product that is ready to be sold, such as "product liability insurance" requirements also described previously, that must be met before many retail outlets will even consider carrying a product. These are the many things to take care of, to get a product ready to launch on the market however, there is another option.

The other option would be to offer the product-invention for licensing, to a manufacturer, who can take care of these issues and simply pay you a "royalty" percentage from sales of the finished product. The name for such an agreement that you would enter into with a manufacturer, is called a "Licensing Agreement".

As the product owner/inventor, you would be the "Licensor", simply meaning the party who grants these rights and the manufacturer entering into such an agreement, to market your product-invention, would be the "Licensee", simply meaning the party who is being granted these rights.

What are the advantages in licensing a product-invention, rather than in marketing it on your own? One major advantage is that all of the above mentioned items, needing to be put in place and completed, in order to get the product ready for marketing, would be at the Licensee's expense. This might exclude the expense for patenting, since most inventors wisely choose to get at least a "patent pending" status (in process of approval for a patent) before exposure of their invention to second parties.

There are some inventors who will actually license their inventions with the condition included, that the manufacturer will also pay for securing patent protection. In cases like these however, it is important to proceed very cautiously and with use of "Non-Disclosure, Non-Use Agreements" that a manufacture would sign prior to viewing the invention.

These type agreements that are signed prior to review of your invention simply state that they agree not to use your invention, in any way or disclose your invention, to third parties, without your prior written consent.

The problem with proceeding without a patent however, is that manufacturers will have reason to question your invention's potential because they may feel that if you are not willing to first patent it, before offering it for licensing, that you possibly don't have a great deal of confidence in the invention. This may cause them to conclude that if you don't believe in it enough to apply for a patent, why should they?

In addition to the advantage of expenses being the manufacturers, other than possibly the patenting, as we have looked at, another advantage, is that all other responsibilities are also the licensee's. They will be responsible for designing attractive packaging for your invention, in getting product liability insurance secured for it and in promoting your product-invention, through ongoing advertising.

The responsibilities in marketing a product are many but the advantage in licensing a product-invention, over marketing it yourself, is the fact that an existing manufacturer, is already set up to accomplish these things. You simply grant the rights, through a Licensing Agreement and are paid a percentage on their sales, for doing so.

It is important, to proceed with a prospective Licensing Agreement, with caution. You must carefully consider and think out every condition and term; you wish to be included in your agreement. Things to consider, are the "royalty percentage" you would be willing to settle for, the "Initial term of Agreement", meaning the length of time you want the initial term to be for, in months or years.

You would also want clauses/articles that protect you from law suits that might arise, from the practices of the manufacturing company. You would also need to be able to terminate the agreement, in the event the manufacturer, did not honor the agreement, due to non-payment of royalties or by not fulfilling a minimum sales requirement, in order for the agreement to remain in force, etc..., but you want to be workable with them and not be so strict as to make them disinterested in entering into a contract to market your product-invention.

Always consider and think these things through carefully and never be so eager as to enter into a binding agreement, without making sure you have covered all bases for yourself and your invention.

CHAPTER SIX

Beware of Dishonest Invention Companies

As a successful Inventor, who began marketing my own product-inventions, in the 1980s, I learned a great deal about how to proceed with a new invention. Unfortunately, some of my lessons were learned the hard way, through negative experience!

One negative experience was with an "Invention Company" but let me say before proceeding further with this article, that not all Invention Companies are bad, some are good but you must proceed with one, with caution, as you will better understand in these next paragraphs.

In 1984, myself, along with my brother-in-law, co-invented a fishing tackle accessory, called "The Rod Floater", a flotation device to keep rod and reel combos from sinking if dropped overboard while fishing. We knew beyond a shadow of a doubt, that our invention had real potential and so we began to seek ways of getting the product-invention marketed.

We found in the ads sections of Mechanics type magazines, ads listing "Inventor Assistance", also called "Invention Companies". Their ads were very eye-catching and impressive and so we chose the best looking one and ordered their info-package.

The package arrived within only a few days and upon opening and reading it, we found there were many implied promises that if we would retain their services, success with our invention was practically around the corner.

We first ordered what they called their "Basic Information Package", for a fee of just under $400.00. Upon receiving this even more detailed info-package, we found that the implied promises for success were even more evident, with their claim of having evaluated our invention and having found tremendous potential in it.

They also detailed where the item could be sold, once in the hands of a Manufacturer they would secure for us, who could produce and sell it.

This would be under a "Licensing Agreement" this Invention Company would negotiate for us.

51

This is a contract that secures a "royalty percentage" that would be paid to us from sales by a Manufacturer. Under this prospect of an agreement, we the invention owners would be called the "Licensor" and the marketing company would be called the "Licensee". Our percentage to be paid on sales, would be from 2% to 5% and would be calculated and paid to us each quarter (four times a year). It all sounded so very exciting!

With all of these possibilities, we went forward with the Invention Companies next step, the phase in which they would attempt to secure such a deal for us and our invention. The cost for this "next step", which we had to finance, was just under $4,500.00, bringing our total fees to the Invention Company, to nearly $5,000.00!

Approximately two years into their supposed efforts to line up a Licensee for us, they notified us by phone that they were in the process of negotiating a contract for us, with a Manufacturer! We were absolutely ecstatic upon hearing this wonderful news!

As we waited eagerly to hear the results of their negotiations, weeks passed and so we finally phoned the Invention Company and coincidentally, they were just wrapping up their meetings with this Licensee, who by the way, had a very impressive, global-sounding name! A couple of days later, we received the news, that the company agreed to pay us 2% quarterly, in exchange for rights to our invention! We were sent the contract to sign and upon rushing the signed copies back to them, we then sat back and waited, knowing that within a few months, we would begin receiving royalty checks!

Once an entire year had passed, with no word, check or correspondence of any kind, we felt it was time to check on the status of our invention's marketing. We called the Invention Company and to our great dismay and huge disappointment, they had the news to report that the Manufacturing Firm that was so interested in marketing our product-invention had merged with another corporation and this new formed firm, was no longer interested in our product and was terminating our Licensing Agreement.

We were so distraught but were encouraged by the Invention Company, that they already had other interested Manufacturers they were presenting our invention to.

As another year of dead silence passed, I presented the idea to my brother-in-law, of pursuing marketing of the invention on our own. He agreed and we began securing investors, whom we could form a corporation of partners with, to get the product on the market. Through our newly formed Corporation, we were able to secure the money-capitol to obtain a design patent for our invention, to get set up to manufacture it, packaging for it and the other odds and ends, such as product liability insurance secured for it, as described earlier.

Once all of these things were in place, we launched our product. We immediately began to experience success, getting the "Rod Floater", into a region of Wal-Mart Stores, then into Bass Pro Shops and Cabela's, plus many other large, reputable retail outlets. We also secured distributors, sales reps and T.V. Marketing.

We also landed a promotional deal with a large Oil Company, who used the "Rod Floater" as a promo give-away, by placing one in their cases of outboard motor oil!

After a couple of years of success, I did a little investigation, to find out what actually happened with our Invention Company misfortune. I first called the Chamber of Commerce, in the City where this company was located, that wanted to market our invention, as the Licensee. The Chamber of that city stated that to their knowledge, no such company ever existed! I also called some of the other companies that were supposedly called on by the Invention Company, during their endeavor to get our invention Licensed and these companies stated that they did not have record of our product-invention, ever having been submitted to them for consideration!

I also found out, that by law, in many states at that time, Invention Companies were required to release a statement detailing accomplishments or achievements they had experienced on behalf of inventors that would include the past five years of their "service" to inventors.

As a former client, I requested one of these from the invention firm and upon receiving it, found they had accomplished a big fat "zero". They had not licensed one single invention, for a client, for the past five years!

My belief is that the supposed licensing of our invention was a bogus happening. I feel they used our product as an example to other inventors they wished to receive fees from, to entice them into becoming clients by telling them they had successfully licensed ours.

How do you protect yourself from scammers such as these? First of all, check their credentials, the best you possibly can. Ask them for references of other inventors they have had success in getting inventions licensed for. Get a Statement of Achievements from them, to see if they have had any successes at all. If they have not, chances are, their profits are made exclusively from fees they charge and not from successfully licensing inventions for clients. You might also consider using an Invention Firm that charges only an expense type fee, with their main profits being made from percentages of royalties they have secured for inventors.

Always proceed with caution and take plenty of time making your decisions because as the saying goes, "haste makes waste".

If I were to express the most important things I've learned, in getting products marketed and licensed, I would say first of all, to other inventors; "Be persistent, even in the face of adversity and pursue your dreams with absolute determination!". I would also warn that there are dishonest people out there, ready to cheat you at every opportunity, so use some wisdom when dealing with that element of the world that is out there and do not make hasty decisions!

(END OF SECTION ONE)

SECTION TWO:

The Best Darn Invention Marketing Book!

Vital Information for the Aspiring Inventor

(NOTE: Chapters within this section cover some of the information that was in the previous section but it was written at a different time and with additional perspectives included.)

CHAPTER ONE

Researching the Market Value of Inventions

Determining the Worth of a New Product Idea

When an invention is believed to have potential for being successfully developed into a marketable product, there are questions that help to determine that evaluation. While an invention can appear to have potential when considered on face-value, it is in an inventor's best interest to research the market potential of a new product idea, the best possible, before investing further time and expense into its development.

There are several basic areas that should be considered in this process of evaluating an invention, as addressed in the subheadings that follow.

Does the Invention Solve a Problem?

This is always a major question when evaluating an invention because solving a problem is the basic purpose behind all inventions. It needs to eliminate a step that adds difficulty in accomplishing something or in making that step easier for those using the invention.

Some of the ways a product-invention helps to solve a problem include the following.

- makes a common task easier
- eliminates a step in accomplishing a task
- adds enjoyment to a task
- provides a convenience when performing a task

If for example an invention is in the area of household cleaning products the invention should solve a problem or add a convenience in that area.

A product that makes it easier to empty a full vacuum cleaner bag, a dishwasher additive that improves the cleaning action on dishes and an attachment for a bathtub-shower cleaning brush that allows reaching better from a standing position, would all be examples of household cleaning products that solve a problem for consumers. If the invention only solves a minor problem that most people are not concerned about, an inventor may feel it is not worth pursuing further. If it solves a problem that is concerning to consumers who are obviously looking for a solution, this may indicate that is has real market value. This is the basic appeal that would create sales and by determining how important it is in solving a problem or adding a convenience, this can also help to determine its potential market value.

Does the Invention have a Wide Appeal?

Even when a product has a definite problem solving ability, this does not necessarily determine how well it will sell on the market. If for example, an invention is a chew-toy for dogs with sensitive teeth that would be very desirable for owners of dogs suffering with this problem.

It does however need to be determined if there are only a small number of dogs who have this problem or if there are potentially large numbers of them.

A company, who already manufactures dog chew-toys, could add this type product to their line and it would possibly be worthwhile for them to do so.

An inventor however would likely only benefit to a small degree should he license the invention (to receive royalty-percentage payments) to a dog chew-toy company due to limited sales compared to products that would benefit all dogs in general.

In these cases an inventor needs to determine the cost to develop an invention into a presentable product for pet toy companies, versus the amount that might be paid in royalties under a License Agreement or for an outright sale of the invention.

If the cost to develop it is not higher than the expected profit that would be made, the invention might be worth pursuing further.

Can the Invention be Manufactured at a Reasonable Cost?

Determining the cost to manufacture an invention consists of materials needed to make a finished product and in the manufacturing process. Some inventions have parts that are already available through other manufacturers and can be incorporated into the finished product, to reduce some of the cost.

If there are however, parts that require special tooling or molds, this must be factored into the manufacturing cost.

If an inventor plans to license his invention and not self-manufacture it, the "Licensee" (company that will manufacture it) can conduct research for using the most affordable materials needed that still retain quality for the finished product.

If an inventor plans to self-market the product-invention, he would still need to have manufacturers helping him, to conduct studies on costs to afford-ably but effectively manufacture a finished product on a timely basis.

Can the Invention be Packaged Affordably?

Packaging is a major factor in both protecting a product from damage and in attracting consumers with sales appeal. Most product-inventions can be packaged for sale feasibly, so that the cost of the packaging doesn't raise the final retail price too high for consumers to afford it. There are however cases in which a product has multiple parts that must be wrapped in protective materials inside of its main container.

Products can also be heavier than average and require stronger, more expensive materials to protect and package them. An inventor needs to determine if he or a manufacturer he may license or sell his invention to, can package his product-invention efficiently and afford-ably, so that it can still be offered at a desirable retail price.

This may require researching the cost of packaging materials and the cost to a manufacturer to complete this packaging, using similar products they already package as a guideline.

Once the cost of packaging is reasonably determined, an inventor must then combine this cost with that required for manufacturing the invention itself, to determine if an appealing final retail for consumers can still be achieved. If one type of packaging cannot achieve this, an inventor may need to look into alternative ways to package his invention.

These questions and considerations are useful in evaluating the worth in pursuing marketing of a product-invention. It is, however, also important to protect the invention as the inventor goes through this evaluation process by making sure they do not disclose details of it to anyone before they have obtained proper patent protection.

CHAPTER TWO

Preparing for Invention Submission

Patent Pending and Production Costs

When an inventor is planning to submit an invention to industry for outright sale or for licensing or to market it himself, there is vital information needed to proceed. Being fully prepared for submitting an invention to companies with potential interest for marketing it or to directly launch a marketing campaign for an invention is very important. The two main areas of importance are protecting an invention and thoroughly researching costs involved in developing an invention for retail sale readiness. These are essential factors needed for new product marketing.

Patent Protection

The U.S. Patent & Trademark Office (USPTO) warns that not obtaining a patent pending status for an invention within one year of public disclosure can result in denial of a patent application.

It is highly recommended that an invention not be disclosed publicly by an inventor before patent protection is in place. While some inventors desire to first see if there is public interest for their product-invention before going the expense of a patent pending, it is very risky business to test-market without one.

Provisional Patent Program

One cost-effective route for protecting an invention that has been made available by the USPTO is the "Provisional Patent Program" (also covered in SECTION ONE). Once an inventor has conducted a thorough patent search on their own or through a patenting agent or attorney, it can then be submitted for a 1-year provisional patent. The cost for small entities (individuals and companies with 500 employees or less) is only $110.00, as of the year 2009. The patent can be allowed to lapse after the initial term with no further obligation or an inventor can resubmit the invention for a full-term patent of 14 years. This gives an inventor time to develop and test market his product-invention before he invests in further patent expenses.

Manufacturing Costs

Having a new product idea can be exciting, especially if the product-invention is unique and will genuinely solve a problem or offer a needed-convenience to consumers who will purchase it. Even if an inventor does not directly sell an invention, having accurate costs figured to manufacture a shelf-ready product with the best possible accuracy is essential.

This is so all levels of markup at the following levels can be calculated as accurately as possible:

- Distributor price
- Wholesale price
- Sales rep commissions
- Final retail

(Note: Some manufacturers choose not to sell to distributors or pay sales rep commissions but strictly sell at a single wholesale price to retailers.)

This will let the inventor know how competitive a finished, packaged product will be on the market.

It is information potential licensees also require (whether researched by them or the inventor) in order to seriously consider marketing an invention under a royalty agreement with a licensor (one offering rights to an invention).

Competitive Final Retail

If the final retail of a new product is undesirable to the consumer, this can override their recognition of how useful the product would be to them because of non-affordability or lack of cost-effectiveness.

Costs may need to be cut back in the following areas to keep the final retail competitive:

- Manufacturing process
- Materials
- Packaging

(Inventors who market their own inventions must also consider promotional and advertising costs.)

This may require research to find the most cost effective sources and resources to obtain best possible prices while retaining a necessary quality and attractiveness for a product-invention.

Having these costs in place can help an inventor go much further when submitting an invention to potential licensees, potential investors and even potential retail store outlets and chains.

CHAPTER THREE

Conducting a Preliminary Patent Search

Searching Online before Securing Professional Assistance

A patent search can confirm the originality of a new invention or reveal that a similar invention has already been protected under an existing patent or patent-pending.

While an inventor can conduct a patent search on his own, there are also patent agents and attorneys who can assist in this for a fee. Searching online can help inventors locate patent search assistance so that it is conducted professionally. This will offer assurance that it has been done thoroughly and completely.

Some inventors may wish to conduct their own preliminary patent search first, before paying for professional assistance. The subheadings that follow can help inventors know how to conduct a preliminary patent search.

Search the Shelves and Catalogs of Retail Outlets

While this step isn't technically part of a patent search, it can help confirm the value in conducting one. It might also reveal to an inventor that no further search is needed if the invention already exists on the market. A more thorough preliminary patent search would not be necessary; if an inventor discovers that his invention or one that is very similar is already being marketed by someone else.

As a first step in establishing the originality of a product invention and in determining if more thorough search is merited, it's a good idea to make sure a product-idea is not already widely available in major chain stores or in major catalog outlets.

Conduct a Search on Major Search Engines

This is a another preparatory step in getting ready for conducting an actual patent search through the United States Patent & Trademark Office (USPTO).

There are websites that are not actually connected to the USPTO, yet still index patented inventions and even non-patented inventions on the search engines, as part of their services to inventors. By conducting an online search on Google, an inventor can better-establish the need to do a more detailed and thorough search on the USPTO website. Google in-fact now has a search engine called "Google patents beta".

Other major search engines in addition to Google include the following:

- Yahoo.com
- Ask.com
- MSN.com
- AolSearch.com
- HotBot.com
- AltaVista.com
- Gigablast.com

If, for example, an inventor believes he has a new, unique type of windshield wiper for automobiles, he can use several variations of search terms that describe the product-invention. It might also yield more results to include the word "patent" in the search.

This step not only helps to locate any pages of patented inventions that might be similar to a new invention, but also displays results on any non-patented products in general that might already be on the market.

A widely marketed product of similar purpose or design might pose too much competition for a new invention and might be a deciding factor against a further search using the USPTO website.

Searching Patents on the USPTO Website

The value in a more thoroughly conducted patent search is in working toward getting patent protection for an original invention by following up with a patent application. But it also helps prevent an inventor from infringing upon another patent which could make them legally liable for damages if it results in loss of sales or threatens the originality of an existing patented invention.

Inventors or their agents/attorneys can go online and visit the "USPTO's Index to the United States Patent Classification System."

This online source of granted patents and patent-pending inventions lists inventions of every kind that have been submitted through applications, in alphabetical categories.

Conducting a thorough patent search, following a preliminary one or even as a first-step toward gaining protection for inventions, takes time but can be well worth the effort to establish the originality and patent-ability of them.

CHAPTER FOUR

The Valuable USPTO Provisional Patent Program

Full Invention Protection for One Year

The U.S. Patent & Trademark Office's - Provisional Patent Program offers patent protection for one year while inventors develop their inventions. This program allows time for establishing the value of inventions, before investing in more permanent type patents. This is an important way to help new inventors reserve more of their funds for invention development, rather than needing more up-front money to invest in patents and before having the opportunity to fully test-market their inventions.

One Year Length Provisional Patents

The Provisional Patent Program (PPP) which was established by the USPTO in the year 1995 has in one sense replaced a former program discontinued by the USPTO that was called the "Disclosure Document Program" (DDP).

The DDP was a method offered to establish an invention's "date of conception" but offered no real protection and was discontinued in the year 2007.

A provisional patent offers an established date of conception for inventions and much more. This includes a trial period for test marketing and selling an invention for one year, before an inventor follows through with one of three more permanent types of patents. Continuing with longer-term patents is optional under the PPP and an inventor may instead allow it to lapse if he feels his invention does not merit further patenting.

The three longer term patents which are 14 years in duration include the following:
• design patents (design for an article of manufacture)
• industrial patents (a new and useful process of manufacture or composition of matter)
• plant patent (new asexually produced variety of plant).

Securing a "Patent Pending" Status

Formerly, when inventors sent their invention-descriptions in to the USPTO under the Disclosure Document Program, they would do so to establish a "date of conception," meaning proof of the date in which they established having invented it. This program, however, was not a protection for the invention as a provisional patent is and also did not allow for the inventor placing the "patent pending" notation on their invention; it's packaging and promotional materials. This is the advantage that the still affordable provisional patent has over the former, lower cost DDP.

A Cost of $105.00 for Small Entities

The USPTO offers provisional patents to small entities, meaning individuals or companies that have less than 500 employees, for a nominal fee of only $105.00 (please check the USPTO website for price updates). This is a very cost-effective price because an inventor is allowed to test market his invention for one year after notification that they have received and accepted a PPP application.

If during the one year, an inventor discovers that the invention does not merit following through with a more permanent patent, at additional costs, he can allow the term to expire and forfeit the option to continue the patenting processes. If an inventor decides his invention is not worth the obtaining of a longer term patent (14 years), he can simply allow the provisional patent to lapse and he will have no further patenting costs or obligations with the USPTO. If, however, the value of the invention is proven during the one year grace period, the inventor may choose to invest further, to obtain a longer-term patent.

Opportunity for License Agreements

A major value of the one-year grace period provided by the PPP is that the worth/value of the invention can be established, with a much-lower risk of theft of the inventor's product-invention. It is also valuable in that an inventor may pursue a licensing (royalty agreement) during the one year grace period.

If any further patenting is done, it would be the responsibility of the "licensee" (if specified contractually).

This means the party paying royalties on sales for marketing an invention under a License Agreement, would be responsible for patent updates, should an inventor ("licensor") secure a licensing for his invention before the one year period has expired.

See the link in the "Sources" section below, that goes to the USPTO webpage, which gives detailed information about the PPP. The page also gives instructions on how to apply for a provisional patent and the address for sending applications and payment, to secure a provisional patent status for an invention.

CHAPTER FIVE

Test Marketing Inventions Effectively

Determining the Potential of New Products

When an inventor has a new invention that he wants to be certain will sell well on the market, he can take steps that help determine the marketability of the invention. Test marketing a new product-invention not only gives potential buyers the opportunity to see how much demand there is for a product, but also gives the inventor the opportunity to determine how much further time and investment an invention merits. It is important before using any of the methods listed in the subheadings below, that an inventor first secure proper patent protection for an invention that will be test-marketed as discussed in the previous chapters.

The Value in Test Marketing New Product-Inventions

The benefits that are accomplished through test marketing product-inventions include the following.

...
- to get an idea of how well a new product will be received by the public
- to see if there is a demand for it in the marketplace
- to determine if there will be repeat customers for a new product
- to gain the interest of buyers at retail chain stores and outlets

Display an Invention at Trade Shows

There are many trade shows that offer booth space for displaying and selling new products. If for example, an invention is in the hardware category, he can look for scheduling of trade shows for hardware products in his area or in areas he is willing to travel to. A great way to find information on trade shows is to go online and use search terms such as "upcoming hardware trade shows". To find ones being held in a particular state or city, one can simply add the name of the city and/or state in the search term. By attending trade shows and displaying a product-invention, one can get an idea of how well it will be received by the public.

This is done by observing how many people attending them stop by a display booth to look at a new product. This also gives the opportunity to ask attendees what they think about a product, if they would use it and if they see any features of the product they would prefer to see modified. After attendance at a number of these type shows, one would then be able to compare notes on them and have a better idea of how the product will be received by the general public, once it becomes available on the market.

Offer a Product-Invention through Telemarketing Sales

There are local cable advertising programs available in most cities that allow one to advertise in a limited area for a lower cost than regional or national advertising will cost. Most of them also offer production services and can produce a semi-professional telemarketing spot for a product-invention.

An inventor would also need to obtain a toll-free ordering phone line, for taking orders, which are now available at a low cost or on a charge-per-call basis.

Some major phone companies that provide basic phone service will also add a toll free phone line to existing basic service at no additional charge.

Some T.V. shows have unsold advertising spots that they might be willing to offer in exchange for a percentage of sales a product generates from an ad. This is called a "P.I." arrangement meaning one agrees to pay the show running the ad a percentage of each sell or "per inquiry" that it generates. By offering a product-invention for sale in a T.V. ad, one is often able to see if there is a demand for it in the marketplace.

Conduct Surveys of Consumers Regarding a Product-Invention

To survey potential buying-consumers, one needs to compose a survey form, with lines for them to sign. The document would simply need to inquire as to whether a consumer would like to see a new product available at their local store. These surveys, once completed, can also be presented to potential buyers of the product whose interest in carrying it in their stores is often heightened by any public interest that is shown.

If one is trying to get the interest of a particular store-chain or outlet, wording the survey so that public interest is shown in seeing a new product specifically available in that store can add to its effectiveness. These type surveys can be conducted at trade shows or booth shows of any kind but can also be conducted at stores where one wants to generate interest. This would of course require that there is permission granted to conduct the survey on the store premises. A large list of consumers signing this type of survey can generate more interest with buyers who see the respondents as potential repeat customers for a new product.

Ask Permission to Test a Product-Invention in Stores

If one is trying to gain the interest of a chain-store for example, an appointment can be made with the corporate buyer and request the opportunity to test a new product in one or up to a few of their stores. If permission to test market a new product in a limited number of stores is granted, it gives an opportunity to monitor the sales, to see if the product can be expanded in the chain.

This of course would be dependent upon how well the test period goes with a product. It might also be a good idea to advertise the new product in the cities it is available in for the test, by placing ads in local newspapers. To gain the interest of a buyer for test marketing a product, one could also offer the new product at a discounted price and let the buyer know that advertising will be obtained for the authorized store(s) during the test.

The preceding subheadings offer general guidelines for several methods that can help determine the market value of a new product-invention. An inventor would however want to proceed with any test marketing, with caution, making sure that public exposure of an invention is done at the best possible timing. It is also important while attempting to determine the sales potential of a new product, that any contracts or agreements involved in the process are carefully considered and researched, which may require the assistance of legal counsel in some cases.

CHAPTER SIX

The Invention License Agreement Option

Receiving Royalty Payments from a Manufacturer

An inventor has two options to choose from to proceed with getting an invention marketed, self-marketing or a License Agreement.

These two options should be investigated and researched if both are being considered. The advantage of self-marketing is in the fact that an inventor has potential to a make a higher profit margin through direct sales of an invention. The advantage in licensing an invention is in the fact that despite a lower profit being made, the expense and labor in the marketing effort is that of the manufacturer obtaining the rights.

Self-Marketing an Invention

With the self-marketing option, an inventor will be responsible for every aspect of the marketing process, from top to bottom. This would include getting the following items completed.

...
- obtaining a patent pending and/or trademark registration
- getting packaging designed and printed for merchandising through retail outlets
- setting up a manufacturing facility or obtaining the services of a manufacturer
- securing product liability insurance required by retail outlets

In order to have a finished, packaged product ready to ship to merchandisers, retail outlets and distributors, these requirements must be met. There are many other responsibilities that must be completed as well, in order to have a product ready for launching on the market. These are the things to consider when looking into the self-marketing option.

The License Agreement Option

The other option would be for the inventor to offer the product-invention for licensing, to a manufacturer, who can take care of these issues and simply pay a "royalty" percentage from sales of the finished product.

The name for a contract of this type that would be entered into is a "License Agreement."

The product owner/inventor would be the "licensor," simply meaning the party granting the rights and the manufacturer entering into the agreement, to market the product-invention, would be the "licensee," simply meaning the party who is being granted these rights.

The Advantages of Licensing

What are the other advantages in licensing a product-invention, when compared to self-marketing? One major advantage is that all of the previously mentioned items, needing completed in order to get the product ready for marketing, would be at the licensee's time and expense. This usually excludes the expense for the first stages of patenting, since most inventors choose to get at least a "patent pending" status (pending approval for a full-term patent) before public exposure of their invention. There are some inventors who actually license their inventions with the condition included that the licensee/manufacturer pay for the securing of a patent pending.

In cases like these however, it is important that an inventor proceed cautiously and with use of "Non-Disclosure - Non-Use Agreements," signed prior to allowing review of the invention. This type of agreement states that the reviewing party agrees not to use the invention, in any way or to disclose it, to third parties, without prior written consent of the inventor.

The problem with proceeding without a patent however is that manufacturers will have reason to question an invention's potential. They may feel that if the inventor is not willing to first apply for a patent pending, before offering it for licensing, that they may lack real confidence in the invention. If the inventor doesn't believe in it enough to apply for a patent, why should they?

The USPTO (U.S. Patent & Trademark Office) offers a 1-year patent pending under the "Provisional Patent Program" at a low cost of $110.00 for small entities (small companies and individuals). With this and the effort of first conducting a patent search or having one completed, the expense of a patent pending can be held down to a minimum, prior to offering an invention for licensing.

The Licensee's Responsibilities

In addition to the advantage of expenses being the manufacturer's under a License Agreement, with the possible exception of a patent pending, another advantage is that all other responsibilities are also the licensee's. They are responsible for designing attractive packaging for the invention, getting product liability insurance secured for it and promoting the product-invention, through ongoing advertising.

The responsibilities in marketing a product are many but the advantage in licensing a product-invention, over self-marketing, is also in the fact that an existing manufacturer is already set up to accomplish these things. An inventor is simply granting the rights through a Licensing Agreement and is being paid a royalty percentage on any resulting sales.

Composing a License Agreement

It is important that proceeding with a prospective Licensing Agreement is done so with caution. An inventor must carefully consider every condition and term they wish to include in the agreement.

Things to consider include the royalty percentage willing to be settled for and the initial term of agreement, meaning the length of time the initial term of the contract is to be for, in months or years. An inventor will also want to include clauses/articles that protect them from law suits of any kind that might arise, as a result of the marketing practices of the manufacturing company.

The inventor would also need to be able to terminate the agreement in writing, in the event the manufacturer does not honor the agreement. Non-compliance can be due to non-payment of royalties or by not fulfilling a minimum sales requirement, in order for the agreement to remain in force, should this be included. Terms would however need to be reasonable and workable and not so strict as to cause disinterest by potential manufacturers in entering into a contract to market an invention.

An inventor can study license agreements through search online and/or consult with an attorney who is experienced in composing and executing marketing contracts.

CHAPTER SEVEN

Pursuing License Agreements for Inventions

Successfully Securing Royalty Payments for New Products

A License Agreement is a contract that an inventor enters into with a marketing company that can manufacture and sell (market) his invention as mentioned previously. The information in the subheadings below can help an inventor know how to proceed with obtaining a License Agreement for his invention. It is important however that an inventor first take steps for protecting his invention under a patent pending before offering his invention for licensing. While this point has been repeated often, this is due to the great importance in not risking loss of rights to an original invention.

Making a Product-Invention Prototype

When manufacturing/marketing companies are approached with a new product idea by an inventor, they prefer to have a working model or sample design submitted to them.

This is called a "prototype" and an inventor can make the sample himself or if it is a somewhat complicated product, he can have a manufacturing firm or machine shop, sewing factory, etc. put one together for him.

It is better if an inventor is able to produce a prototype on his own if possible because this reduces the chances of early exposure of an invention and will save on the expense of having a prototype made by a manufacturer.

If an inventor has to use an outside source to get a sample (prototype) made, he should have them sign a "Non-Disclosure Non-Use Agreement," which is an agreement that simply states that upon disclosure of the invention to them, for the purpose of producing a prototype, they agree not to publicly disclose the invention to third parties or to make any further samples of the product for their own use.

The inventor has them sign such an agreement so that they do not expose an invention publicly sooner than it is ready to be launched onto the market.

Invention Submission Materials

It is important to look as professional in the efforts to secure a licensee/manufacturer as possible. An inventor needs to have a professional looking letter of request that is sent out to interest companies in seeing a presentation of a product/invention, with a letterhead at the top of it that includes contact information for interested parties.

It is important to put together the best submission materials possible. These type items can include the following:

- A brochure that describes and highlights an invention
- a demonstration video
- a chart that can be pointed to and referred to
- printed results from any positive test-marketing that has been done.

In other words, anything that presents an invention to a reviewing company in the best possible light is a good thing to have with when making a presentation for an invention.

License Agreement Proposal

Most manufacturers that express interest in an invention want the inventor to set their desired terms so that they can make a final consideration before entering into a License Agreement to market an invention. Manufacturers like to see inventors who know what they want out of their invention rather than having an inventor say to them, "Whatever you guys think." They prefer to have a more detailed proposal placed in front of them so that they can negotiate from that point.

An inventor can find a local attorney to help them compose a License Agreement proposal or they can find one on the internet using a search term such as "sample license agreements," etc. Once one has a general contract in hand, they can customize it to their liking.

The most likely term/condition that requires some time in negotiating with a licensee is the amount of royalty they will be required to pay on units sold for an invention under a licensing. Royalties paid on inventions can vary but according to some sources, a majority of inventions that are licensed receive a royalty between 2% and 10%.

These suggestions can help an inventor to generally know how to pursue and prepare a License Agreement but one factor that is also of great importance is an inventor's ambition. A positive attitude and confidence in pursuing a License Agreement for an invention is a key factor. Inventors who remain confident, ambitious and who don't give up if they initially fail to interest the companies they first make presentations to, are the ones who succeed in eventually getting their inventions Licensed, to receive royalty payments from.

CHAPTER EIGHT

Methods for Licensing Inventions

Preparing New Product Submissions and Presentations

The advantage for an inventor in licensing his invention is that a manufacturer, marketing company will agree to pay a small royalty percentage on sales they achieve. Companies that are potential licensees can be found by looking in magazines or catalogs that feature products by companies that are within an invention's field of industry or one can go online and search using terms on search engines that describe an invention and find companies that way. It is important to secure a patent pending before presenting an invention to manufacturers for licensing consideration.

Research Potential Licensee-Companies

The manufacturing/marketing company an inventor licenses his invention to, is called the "licensee" and the inventor or his agent is referred to as the "licensor."

If an invention is in an industry such as pet supplies, fishing tackle, health & beauty aids, etc., then one simply gathers information on companies that are in the invention's field of industry, so that those who look reputable can be contacted about reviewing the new product-invention.

The advantages in securing a License Agreement for an invention include the following:

• Ongoing royalty payments
• marketing expenses are the licensee's
• an established company can gain wide exposure for inventions
• product liability and patent-related legal issues are the licensee's responsibility.

Following Up on Invention Submissions

When methods used for locating potential licensees yield lists of companies that look to be high quality and reputable in their industry, one can then contact them by written letter or by email to request an opportunity to submit an invention to their new product buyer.

One can then either follow-up on letters/emails with a phone call or it can be requested that contacted companies reply to the letter sent, to confirm receipt of it and/or interest in a more detailed submission. The advantage of mailed letters is that they can be sent return receipt, so that an inventor knows it was received, on a specific postmarked date.

It is usually more effective to state in a letter or email that it will be followed up with a phone call. When one receives responses from manufacturers interested in further reviewing an invention, one can either send a product sample/prototype and further written details about the invention or request an appointment to present the invention in person at their buying office.

Rehearsing and Timing Invention Presentations

A presentation should be practiced before making one in person. An inventor should be well prepared to make a presentation for their invention but should also insure that the presentation is timed, so that it does not exceed a reasonable time limit.

A presentation generally should not exceed 20 minutes in length because executive buyers with manufacturing companies are usually extremely busy and a shorter presentation can be effective and is usually the best approach. A buyer can extend the length of a presentation if he chooses to, by asking questions after an inventor is done with the initial presenting.

Composing a License Agreement Proposal

An inventor should compose a sample license agreement that shows all of the terms and conditions that need to be included in the contract, leaving certain terms blank, such as the amount/percent of royalty that will be paid and the length/term of the contract in years that it is initially in force. Having a proposal on-hand gives an inventor the readiness to negotiate terms, should a presentation meeting reach that stage of interest by a buyer.

License Agreement Terms and Conditions

An inventor may wish to set the term that a License Agreement is in force with a manufacturer (length of time).

This can be for only one or two years for example, with an option for renewal at the end of the term. This way, renewal depends upon the initial sales performance of the licensee. An inventor might also wish to include the condition of minimum sales that are accomplished per contract year by the manufacturer/licensee. It might also be a good idea to include a clause in the contract that gives both inventor/licensor and the licensee the right to terminate the license agreement. This offers both parties a protective clause in the event for example that the licensee fails to pay royalties at the set contractual time periods or for other legitimate reasons. A licensee might also respectfully terminate a License Agreement in the event they feel they would be unable to fulfill their obligations, so that the inventor/licensor can pursue better options.

Requiring Timely Royalty Payments

The royalty payment conditions can require royalties, to be calculated and paid, quarterly (4 times a year) or monthly, etc...

Should the licensee become past-due in making royalty payments (by 10, 15 or 30 days, etc.); the licensor has the option to terminate the contract in writing – such as with a 15 or 30 day notice.

Inventors should take their time in pursuing License agreements carefully. Being in too much of a hurry to license an invention can result in bad decisions when entering into contracts that are binding and that must run their full terms unless terminated due to violations of terms. It is in an inventor's best interest to fully consider his options when entering into a License agreement and to do so with the help of an attorney if necessary.

CHAPTER NINE

My Invention Marketing Success Story Revisited

My Experience in Self-Marketing and Licensing Inventions

In the early 1980s, I co-invented a fishing tackle accessory, an attachment for fishing rod and reel combos with my brother-in-law. We named the product-invention "The Rod Floater". We saw the need for an invention that floats fishing rod and reel combos, after having near-drowning experiences with our own rod combos and after hearing the stories of other fishermen who had lost their own rod combos to watery graves, never to retrieve them. This inspired us to also add the catch phrase to the Rod Floater packaging; "A Life Vest For Your Fishing Rods"! The Rod Floater is a very simple device, an 8-inch, cylinder-shaped piece of poly-foam material, similar to what you see water noodles and Nerf type toys made from, that attaches to fishing rods, just above the rod handle, in the space above the fishing reel and just below the first rod eyelet.

We knew our invention had potential for the reasons I've stated plus the fact that children learning to fish and fishermen who are physically challenged are also at risk for dropping their rod combos overboard. To top it all off, my father-in-law had lost one of his own rod combos overboard, while trolling and having his fishing line snag on brush in the lake, which flipped his rod over the side, never to be retrieved in the deep water. With the Rod Floater, we knew that such mishaps would not end in tragedy because with our product invention, rods dropped overboard, would float on top of the water, allowing for easy retrieval of rod combos.

We eventually came out with Rod Floaters in bright yellow and orange, in addition to basic black so that fishermen are also able to spot rods dropped overboard, even at a significant distance. The bright colors are handy if a rod is dropped from a speeding boat and you have traveled a distance before being able to turn around and retrieve it or if your rod is pulled overboard by a fish and he swims across the lake with it. Since marketing the Rod Floater starting in 1990, we have actually received product-testimonial letters from fishermen.

This includes some from pro fishing guide services who were grateful to retrieve their rods after experiencing these very scenarios I have just described.

My Negative Invention Company Experience

My brother-in-law and I at the time were not familiar with the concept of invention companies but only had basic knowledge about them from seeing their ads in mechanics magazines. We decided we would contact one of them and request information. The one we contacted was one of the more publicized companies and upon receiving their information, we sent our invention concept to them in detail, on paper.

They responded back to us promptly, assuring us that our invention had very broad potential. We decided to go with this invention company and paid for a "basic information package", which consisted of them providing us a folder with market-potential estimates for our invention and professional line-art graphics, depicting our invention.

Upon receiving this basic information package, the invention company strongly suggested that we enter a contract with them, for a second step they would then undertake, to present our invention to industry for licensing it and if a licensing were successfully accomplished, we would receive royalty payments from sales of our product-invention. We did enter this second phase of their services, with a cost to us of several thousand dollars, the basic information package having already cost us several hundred dollars.

Beware of Invention Company Scams!

Let me say at the start of this paragraph in regard to invention companies, that not all of them practice bogus or false services, just to get fees from inventors but some invention companies are legitimate and sincere. In our case however, the invention company we entered into a contract with, was not completing the services they claimed to be providing. We were able to determine this, by contacting many of the companies they claimed to be making submissions of our invention to and these companies made it very clear to us that they had never received the submissions.

At one point, the invention company also claimed they had found a corporation interested in marketing our invention and they eventually entered into a licensing agreement with them to market our invention. We were actually provided contracts to sign, in order for this corporation to manufacture and market our product-invention.

After more than a year following our signing of the licensing agreement, with no word from the invention company or the corporation/licensee, we inquired with the invention company as to the status of their marketing and were told that the corporation merged with another company and this newly-formed entity no longer wished to continue with the license agreement!

We were devastated to say the least and at that point, asked for a release from the remaining time/term of our contract with the invention company and they granted us the release. The lesson to learn from this example is to thoroughly investigate an invention company, their reputation, references and past history, before contracting with one to assist you with your invention!

A few months after the release from our contract with the invention company, I called the Chamber of Commerce in the city and state where this corporation who entered the license agreement with us was located. I was told that no such company ever existed and that if it had, regardless of their claimed merge with another company, they would have known about them. This confirmed my suspicions that began long before we asked for the release from our contract with the invention company, that they were indeed a bogus inventor's help-resource and not a legitimate invention company.

While I cannot give the company's name for obvious legal reasons, I will add that this experience having occurred over 20 years ago, could mean that the company has since reformed and may now be operating legitimately. Then again, they may still be scamming sincere inventors out of their hard earned money to obtain illegitimate fees. If an inventor is determined to go the invention firm route, he should check for complaints against a company being considered, at the Better Business Bureau website.

There are also inventor information sources online, that actually list companies that are known to have committed scams. By conducting a search on Google or other search-engines using the term "Inventor Fraud", many pages of sources will appear that supply lists of companies to avoid. There is in fact one such resource called The National Inventor Fraud Center (NIFC) that directs inventors away from scam companies and toward any that are honest and reputable.

Despite our negative invention company experience, we eventually licensed the Rod Floater, in 1996 and have received monthly royalty checks from that time, to date. Some inventors prefer licensing to marketing on their own, which I have given detail-to, in the previous chapters. Before getting the wonderful licensee we now have, we previously got the Rod Floater into Wal-Mart stores (regionally), Bass Pro Shops, Cabela's, Academy Stores, telemarketed on national T.V. shows and a national promotional premium deal with a major oil company, who promoted their outboard motor oil, using Rod Floaters as a giveaway in cases of the boat motor oil in the year 1992.

I invented and developed five other products in the outdoors sports industry and was able to get four more of these into Wal-Mart stores regionally as well before selling the products out-right to a company who still markets these as well.

It is my sincere wish that this ebook contributes to the success of many other inventors who help to give our world a brighter future through new and innovative inventions!

(END)